One-UnPoetry
and other poems

Ayan Chakraborty

BlueRose ONE
Stories Matter

First Published in June 2022

ISBN: 978-93-5628-056-4

BLUEROSE PUBLISHERS

www.BlueRoseONE.com

info@bluerosepublishers.com

+91 8882 898 898

Cover Design:

Aveek

Typographic Design:

Rohit

Distributed by: BlueRose, Amazon, Flipkart

Dedication

To the one who says about this life and beyond...

Acknowledgement

This work would not have been possible without the constant support of my parents to whom I owe much more than any poetry can express. I remain indebted to the professors at the Centre for English Studies at Jawaharlal Nehru University, especially Professor Dhananjay Singh, for inspiring me to think beyond what is said and what is given in language. I share my extreme gratitude to Arion Mitra, friend and a great photographer, for the cover design of this book.

I am grateful to my friends and colleagues for their encouragement and inspiration. On retrospect, I feel blessed for the rigorous discussions we have had on and about sentiments and opinions.

Most importantly, I thank the divine Muse to bestow upon me glimpses of poetic instinct from time to time. Those moments of catharsis have led to the book you have at hand.

Preface

"For last year's words belong to last year's language//And next year's words await another voice..."

"Four Quartets" by TS Eliot

This quote from Eliot is all that can be said about poetry. Poetry, as essence of an expression, of art and literature, aesthetics and realism, belongs to the purest domain of creation. It has always been about communication but more about those impressions which cannot be communicated. This 'non-communicable' process contains the most intense of meanings; those experiences that are most elusive in words and real in living.

My tryst with poetry had been an ordinary one in the beginning. Like most, I loved the play of rhyme and the curiosity of words. As I took up literature as my chief academic discipline, I observed more, thought more, and expressed less. This problem of meaning and language, the search for the 'exact' words that define nuances bothered me and at times bogged me down. This is when TS Eliot's works appealed to me. His inclination to paint images and not be overt with sprawling emotions and bending language was a great relief. After all, poetry is often present in prose works too; just like in paintings and sculptures, designs and imaginations. So, the lack of words can be surpassed by impersonal images. Though these ideas drove my first interests in trying my hand at poetry, I realised that sometimes, images confine language. Language needs to flow, no matter how sprawling and untamed they might look like. So, this collection of poems has both moments of impersonal drives and the thoughts of semi-conscious language. There are poems of varying length; some moves on and on; others seem to be short and abrupt.

To conclude, these poems are straight from my experiences and sensations that follow them. It might require re-reading verses to speculate about what they mean but then, I convince myself, that my readers will create meanings and absurdities where I stop short. I wish my readers a great read.

Contents

Pure

Fear grips
where spaces melt into overdone forms
and talks revolve around prickly bears
like excess oil spilt on regular canvas.
The chafing of the sore
under fierce winter light, the cat's sleep is
a cancer of the senses
on a pulley lift and a U V box in the room
where we sanitise our souls in green digits.
It's almost summer and I am afraid to wax my fingers off the cover. My belly is round; it bloats with too much of sand from the child.
I sketch in terror. Sleepy and sure.
Of profane models, peaceful and pure for the mild.

Conditions

The window has been a secret haunt for life this dark winter.
Like it takes me into space of webs and nests, dry pipes and palm fronds,
of squirrels that rake in clothes and cotton;
silently nurturing death in making home. Like you and I did every winter.
Our lights burn on, long into the nights when peacocks mourn the death of a home; you looking into your palm-lines and I creating stories out of it.
My stories were all built on your silences. Look! how the cobwebs hide the sketches we had torn
Like dreams falling with the snow in splinter. They bury the warm afternoons
with subtle finger touches. The squirrels remained silent as lifeless.
Till it grew warmer and the silence was deafening and you chucked out the little life that we thought never existed.
Your palms are white and the window is open. We are still. A squirrel groans like your pulses. Time to time. Hour to hour.

The Birth of a Story

Exhaustion
Or
Urge,
some strange narration
and
a terror of birth-pains.
Remembering a wild coupling within a mid-spring afternoon
that leaves no trace of conception.
Like how topographies segue into each other
on tiring train journeys
with no pride of being
and all you know
is just a change of names
for the states and the councils.
Or, how rooms change their smells
secretly
when you return after an age of distraction;
the doors small, the corridors smaller.
These are stories laughed out of joint.
Free and untrue to science.

The banks that look on burning bridges bring letters
fit to stack up
under the lens of your lamp's surprise.
Revise them. Bear the dehiscence.
The cramps for the sheaf of searching
into newer births.
Failed story-telling are your lived experiences.
Stories that love and belie.
Stories that take more of gravy to the grave.
They fail your failures like forgotten vocabulary.

Keeping Up.

Lights get darker at mornings in my eyes.
Greying curtains and my turning of the screw
into afternoons that rain with it, this dreaming month.
I quiet my alarms and mend a bulleted door to watch some news
on louder evenings. Or peep out.
To feel stories out of thick windows along tremors of sweat and
smell the black of their movements each night.
My room remains dark, darker than Ebenezer Scrooge.
Exacting revenge on my rods, I blind out shadows myself,
laughing.
Damn, the tremor and the shriek!
It's a way of keeping up with my neighbours.
No, not a trick!
None but to drop some news.

Failings today

I had read a lot of poetry tonight.
Searching for truce…
This moment. The next moment to come.
Every moment.
Not the vain kind but one true,
the one without the ruse.
It was a messianic exercise to feel.
Choices proper; to live or to kill.
Dropping down words to read;
reading them aloud
like some inner tension of a seed.

I learnt to drop my desire, thwart a will.
Twenty times today.
He asked about it.
About the time to live, the time to kill

He said, "to be conscious is not to be in time."
I jotted it down too.
Seeking temporalities in a body which lives
I mocked him the best
tracing on Descartes's doubtful conviction, his clichéd test;
But now, I had said:
"If it's a body, it's a noise that you hear and feel but know not if it means anything before it is dead".
Acts at misprision
like a hooked cross freeze within birth, in the nest.
I think nothing.
I tell in jest: "To be conscious is to fix within the clock. Not a stop or a run or a leave or some infirmity from a pest;
that leaves you hollow before you hollow it."
The noise and the body are the uses of my failings.
You know it already.
You pretend to sleep.
You look blind.
You stare at my face to live in haste.

Once upon a dream

To sleep in time
I talk in real
that real in the dream
holding me to time
on uneven keel;
things were never enough but not with this.
Not this much.
Here. More.
This slinking away to time
slobbering out. Like one or three.
Totting out
switching tack,
parring things down to mime.
I won't be sleeping in this sense of that real.
This is our song I will be singing now.
A song where dreaming is more important
than the real. So, bring me back to time.
Once again. This will be a story of a kingdom.
It's not a story in time.
Let's get to it then. A story you would like.
Once upon a dream.

Escape

Skin, like scratches
condense into sickening winter,
like the little water drops thrown out of dense space
breaking webbed Siberian glasses
as it rains tombstones of ice.
There's a city you return to
in violent strides. To find how much porcelain weighs
in cheap bazaars selling contraband.
There you absolve fallen strings.
And the music they share each December
like a ritual. The haunting tune and it's jilted shape.
These are words of deliverance.
To each its own gig. To each its own shock.
To each its own madness from where it once thought to be saved.
To dream's sick recovery.
To each its own escape.

May be, in an early winter.

How difficult it is
to just wake up
in the middle of it all
Staring
and lost
without knowing what it takes,
or how it slept lately
in the innocence
of talking.
The commerce
to keep alive, to warm again
before a cold festival of lights.
That sung about returning in glory.
Or sometimes it changes to describe.
The part of moving away in one such trope. May be.
Maybe it's not just the change
in the flipping months
of wintry skies and the man
and the tilt in the tint of crops and colours.
There's more to performance made after a prep.
They say change is dramatic. Truly.
May be not always.

Brittle, as it is, too in all its strength.
A symptom of lost literature.
But from liquid voices to counting days,
I think to change a grip.
So, I ask you today.
Isn't it quaint, how you and I?
bewitch ourselves and
belittle the play
to measure distances out of silence?

Homecoming

There was time to cross my sleep,
the numbness, the ripple, the winds,
the dance,
the moist in the deep.
I have known to shrink before I had you
And so, I had played a dirge
Calm and full to the dizzy halogen lights
To break out a chunk of that pumping machine floating by old, salty fluids.
It was a question of moving on.
A question of returning back.
A peril of circling around.
Years like courier boxes I had put together. In the skin without the meaning.
So, I dreamt along.
But now, Odysseus to Hamlet, they had risked their return.
So must I today.
Cruising between the hearth and the exile.
It's another homecoming, with a mask.
A story of a mask under the sun.

Squinting

Brushes of thoughts
and
sculptures of pain
there's
dreams of the living
beside
that old mark in your brain

I got
palms humid like dying summer diving into yellow pages,
raiding and raping, looking for ochre traces
while yours tremble
poring over nicely cut overtures of sound.
Recalling history to disgust is an art of our living.
That we do before it rains
And before we choose our way into the mud.
You close your eyes and sing and slip.
I dig too deep and drown and sink.
We love the smell of sewage as clean as the holy water that
they give you at altars of peace.
We disconnect on every space and love at the impossible.

"*Charaiveti, charaiveti*" till we live and forgive.

So before arctic nights, we sing " if you desire healing, fall ill, fall ill..." like the tortoise.

Scared smiles and weak pants.

Living long.

Secure under the daylight of the eclipse.

The First Mark

Twilights fall free fast in September.
Autumnal mornings spent between dark curtains, sleepy, vexed and soundless.
Still on silenced evening beds, your sleep within mine.
Slow noon.
I wake up with a haunting dream of writing in the diasporic.
My room of ocean green scratches a deeper mark
on your walls; there it cuts the filtering light on your face. I count, at once, to suit fine.
I croon.
And feel the sense of the sound, really quick.
Like you do too
with your quivering ambitions that I catch every lost night.
On rooftops, we climb to look beyond spaces of disgust.
Staring at possible shadows, of hunters and the hunted, the thrill and the fright.
Into clouds, before dawn.
Where the floor turns white with your mumbling. We softly whisper words that break the laden crust
of our souls.
Some lives are carved out of Ghibli tales in autumn.
And I fall. Fall beyond reality and respite.
Into the year's consciousness. Into the ocean green of your mark, this, first September.

Pebble Picking

To move between forest alleys is fun.
Knowing that hours darken before monsoon
winds sink in with the grey.
Of their hearts.
Or say,
sleeping on motions that straight hit bogs of death and pr(e/a) y
for survival
or again on another day
whistling the Camus quote and walking into prisons of wild
disgrace.
Come roars or whispers, to feign as they may.
You need to pick up a path before it's too late
and chant Frost's name.
Someone told me at another time to learn.
To learn to pay.
That you give your all and a knife, and learn still to pay
For the blood you keep and the nights you stay.
Awake. Or in a dream when you drown by the seashore
collecting pebbles against boulders. And weigh.
The enormity of life in bits and in colours.
That sink in the fight but remain. Colored. Tiny. Living.
Undead like rocks that float by the bay.

Sense of the Past

Hunting hunted
there are dreams that feel like folded pages of a lost book
which needed re-reading.
Bold letters that I messed up with blind blots and hid between scripts.
Straight out of the Babel without the pride.
Nights are deaf where you feel one voice treads over all others.
This invisibility is a spark in transit,
trying to tell life exists in bleak illustrations
but making it darker all the same.
There's a present less safe than sublimity.
And a past working through fingers only in senses.
In you and me this midnight.
Of you in me till dissolution.

Swing

The last night when I walked on the cobbled lane,
it rained again. I knew it's time.
Things look old often when they bleakly begin.
On the verandahs and at the attics. Lurking between broken walls of comforting unease.
Generations of laughter now framed into broken hourglasses.
Books that had in them what families would mean.
It had rained heavily then too.
There had been plenty of growth in the green.
And the afternoon heat waxed and waned with silly salt potions.
Long days, deep like artic summers, bright but breathlessly long they had been.
There's life lost and regained. Like Milton's paradise.
Now, the numbers have dwindled, new sprouts bask in newer hours, unseen.
There's no death before you locate one in your senses.
And about life?
Less losses, even lesser bouts to win. These are days when rooms smell like apparitions and melodies creak on those few seats. The pain of birth from coyly painted swings.

Shutting

This year, again, I fancied looking beyond the dust showers.
The red from rear of the traffic, the clammy hint of moisture on the windshields and the little hands that keep on striking window glasses.
Lovely little hands with screeching voices. Dark, bruised and beautiful on the glass plates.
Glasses that divide dreams. Glasses that are called brittle. Glasses that are quaintly like unattended time.
They had tiny rings tied to threads on their fingers. Blue and green and yellow. Round page-markers that they called 'ignorance'.
I wondered what they meant.
"Ignorance does not take effort, dada, ignoring does. Place this in your books; it will be a good day"
They shut their mouths, like they shut their hands,
the wind blew in, mildly, sprinkling dust over shut shutters of shops.

Tired

There is nothing more tiring than being tired of oneself.
Of doing it right and yet doing it wrong.
Of moving out and putting it back together.
And yet losing it on every even day.
Knowing the right thing and yet doing it wrong.
Losing out, losing in. Talking. Listening.
Tired. Very tired.
The loops breaks after it forms a new chain. Simmering and malignant.

Sleep

There are nights that are patiently visible.
On terrace roof, in clinging gates. Elbows sticking out wide.
Uncluttered poise. Soaked raindrops growing into sweat beads.
I lapse into the bed-roll, with littered ambitions.
Above your ideas and below your words,
there is so little distance that remains
to question your being. That you stay awake for inking clouds
and count out stars. Here, to grow is to dream living. To move is
to feel. It was a no blues Monday.
To know is to sleep.

Revisits

To begin before things, end,
to look up and let loose
to trail upon years now
and rehear the shivaree
of those days I have safely bracketed into notoriety.
There was plenty in my mind and in your voice today.
I remember I had told you things take time for the centre to hold
and to choose between Yeats and Eliot on a flimsy day like this.
So, I read across pages right after your call and wondered, "was it
you that I had sliced from it..."
that you, the one I sang with at odd dawns, the one I had
partaken of in corners I still don't see light into;
save the dank albums that still clog my last cell.
There were so many shades in those clingy notes I had stamped
upon
and looked lost at coffee shops right between slow jigs.
Music, mind; music against my mind.
The ones I have with me today are the only ones with the quick
beats, they tune

just like the way my pulses throbbed tonight.
It's to Neruda's toast again and my speakers aren't on.
There can't be time to think or to feel, to know to space out of
situations or to write through my vein, again today.
Even when there's poetry in my soul and ink on my hands.
My pages don't sleep back as letters look straight to be born.

Sliced

Summers have long days,
for you to lay back on the bed and snort emptiness
from the hour glass.
The contemplative contour of the street
running into zipped mouths,
gazes that ponder over roof tops
and back
at your limewashed ceiling.
Your drooping spirit like the fan that hangs
between time and durée.
Your heart is as old as compost
like soot on the blade ends, darker at the edges
and layered in between.
Like the way you think of events of the other day. A morale of
collision. Id and ego? That same story?
The fan that hangs a life also hangs a tale.
There are trials. To shape round. To complete.
Your sliced mind, always in transit on a path towards circuitry.
There, like the blades, a whole in their fiercest reverie. Wings
stretching to touch each other, to live the life, to enact the story.
Summers are uncannily long. Like the bottomless
full of your mind.

Topo-nullius

They say about the idea of life, of *polis* and police
of law and language,
of *muthos* and *telos*;
Of seeds that speak,
of violence that erupts, and those moving rationale within drives and eros.
I, too, have tried to pore over these lofty terms with a false sense of pride;
like the one you feel at webinars chanting 'alterity' and 'discourse'.
With passion and life-affirms.
I have tried to drink glee with a glass and look within the writ points of history,
their sites and pauses dreaming in between,
what it takes to form disciplines without causes.
There has been so little change since Plato's three-layered souls or the Stoic 'assent'
Marxist ethics or the post-modern descent into the never-ending celebration of the Pyrrhonian skeptic ethos.
And that now that I sing books are books are books are books
to look away an eye from an eye, a word from a word,
things aren't philosophy within spaces of conquest,
and I live on to battle and beat a struggle against thought and topos.

Dust

These days are heavy, of rains and red skies
I turn out boxes, trade on colours, take in bouts under lone
footlights. There's so much to glean, the mess, the truth
look yellow in the heart and dust red mute.
Aren't you tired of camouflaging? Heard this so many times?
In books and movies, stand ups or sit coms,
must be sea sides?
damn the cliches of thought, sprouts and fungus,
it repeats what it hears sticks to the same,
pukes the draught; there's molten skies now,
the red wore off I tried talking to the bed,
to the beat to languages, I speak but would not know to ideas I
learn,
I smile, I care and will not sow.
This dust is a terrible thing, they are clean, they gel, they sleep.
Live and dream. Yawn and fear.

Blue

The breeze floats beyond the gilt
and whispers interludes that spread nought
when you, unawares, seep in her blushing ambiguities
or his daunting antinomies of thought. Listen as they speak.
That the blue is the same for the calm and the storm and the
shunya is still the same you mock at to
build your barn and your crematorium.
You discard philosophies in your sleep. He wakes up glum in his
walk and knows not the real, the *sphota* and the *cit*. She promises
there is more to it.
She seeks through flags and banners, scurries through absurd
corners of her street, she trembles through
the writhing of the mind, of fleeting consciousness and
her blue feet.

Dying

Wheeling in senses through short breaths of calm,
time warps and calls divide when
your pitch of intelligence unknowingly frames life into an 'it'.
The night slows and we greet them before sleep,
their bouquet of presence dying into a still look.
I wrap languor like a shawl when fire spreads and voices shiver.
When calls vibrate between is and was, I pick up your book.
Chanting humid lines to scoot across terrains of consciousness.
Nerves as fiddle strings are mute or deaf beings.
The photos glimmer like the rectangular square of your
street light
till it catches webs of gossamer threads and peep
in moments of uncertainty.
Death has a strange green smell. Those that beat
within blots of red and salt
and horrors at huts and hospitals glance wide within your
rounded palm.

In A Bar during a Pandemic

On a crowded rally of a pandemic where I had chosen to hide
and miss the blow and shelve morning news like yoga-*asanas*
with a toss,
round my neck and a curved spine, being too
curved for just a flex,
there are views from just a blood-gripped head.
Down where my head almost courts my feet,
I look through sinister roads and decide to call abjection as
infirmity.
I sometimes think I had broken it somewhere back then.
Between measuring urban distancing and a pandemic's creed
nothing much changed. Save a knock on the cell where the once
willful belligerence
turned into guilt reckoning with death and dearth. And soon
after, ignoring began flirting with ignorance through stranger
mirth.
Or say, when the theatre of absurdity moved through the
absurdity of meeting at our theatres. She had said then.
She had said things expand before they contract. Like "...writing
poetry has been a lonely fare to be heard but from afar."

And so, she said, "decide on the 'to...s' first". To look from afar or talk from afar.

But here now, a drowsy mumbling of words brews out of me like the untouched drink fading into myself; now with her gone.

Deeper at a space of shrieks and sighs where my spine broke long back.

Where I learnt the art of loving from afar. There's no to two words now, without an audience and a tapped, neglected tune of yesteryears.

My eyes have been squinting free, close. Near and far.

With none to look at, in a moving dream, alone in a bar.

Think

Bid the glass empty.
While you drop your drink.
Within turns in love, hate and apathy
over
a wrong text at midnight
or
between rude modicum of work
and
a half-betrayed thought,
breathe.
Beyond
blindness to her faults
and
deaf chords of trial
learn to weave tales of future
smoothing the red cover.
This struggle isn't real.
Hold up the mask and miss the blink.
Feel the blues.
Look up still.
Pause the watch
as you slowly let your conflicts shrink.

Outgrowth

There's the drizzle that relieved the forests today.
Ranciere's forest of symbols. An artwork of draining ties.
I blank down my laptop screen and remember Yeats. Says
diseased minds must pour out notoriety. Like the great
rumbling skies
after a few months' sour gulps throw up on crawling sheets
stained between memory and oblivion. The bed is moist for
growth and Plath's pain.
This smell breathes organic on misbegotten tissues that
I spell as memoir. I look out for glimpses in gain,
within the trademarks of sap
I had slowly spilled in the shower. My words swell before
noon as things mean so little, so plain but
take up whole nights of ease to refill the lost comic vein.
In voids. And there, now, to live, I feign.
Putting up with bits of strawed out intelligence on dark
leaves on the shore, at a summer night, by the bay

Shouldn't

Fifteen years back, in some school cell
with long shadows flooding the question floor
Hours moved between rattling lead.
Two faceless glass panes. Standing out of time. They wanted to prise out what I already knew.
To put them in language. Definitions they yell.
To frame the right words. Scary like the handmaid's tale.
I pored over thick books and wrote and rewrote what I already knew.
I erased to fit in right words which they said were only a few.
Till my pages tore black. Till meanings drew in words and blew in me the lack
which it didn't. My language has stitched many faces since. The way I use it hidden on video calls today. Still.
Splitting my roles between hours
I walk up nights like this to feel
what I couldn't.
I try let meanings move and language crack. Turn and watch.
Smile and write. Of wrong words and queer tunes that your truth hear wouldn't.

Invasion

Writing without a mind and sketching into the past
Filling the canvas with swathes of green,
erasing the blunt edges of lead and patching up mistakes
with splashes of white.
Creepers that twine out at last slinking onto territories it coveted.
A capite ad calcem, where you dine, on the bed.
Doodling with hands that respire tawny bits of broken limestone.
The fort is down, the phantom still. As it drivels aloud stories of
dust and wobbles past glare.
A million boots that had darkened laying bare of acrylic before it
could colour expanses.
The lowering of the gates, another chapter of Trojan will but not
quite mistaken this time.
The phantom still lingers past the ruins at breezy nights.
Learning blackened arts of tantra and carbon-dating to peep
into any life of the fort.
He sheds his body after every chapter in gore. He has shed
many bodies since then.
Sometimes on horseback, sometimes defending the gates.
Stinking exhaustion thrown in swamps that now stores his bones.
Selling his parts and his whole to those tales of yore
Where births are unwilling and ends are festivals of growth
alone. .

Find.

This absence of words is a sublime thing
Both at the emptiness of souls and its flow till the brim
These are times when you know not the tread
But you know your eyes dream heavy as lead even before it has made you
A subject in its bed but has bestowed you with the shade that keeps away the scorch.
These are times you know your life now hangs on the edge without the trim.
This absence of words doesn't come from a whim or a fling.

It's about that which quench without expiring
Like the needle that spins on and on without undoing what it makes, and yet you go on looking at the threads
Are they suppling enough to break?
These are times you rely on shallow water beds to plunge into the deep.
So, what if your voices shake?
It's not your quiver alone now that takes
The flames that burn without flaring.

So, I will stand on the soul I touch
Back and forth, here and there.

Spring Again

Every spring,
with the indecisive blow of southern winds
and the melting of dews,
the opening up of blinds the madness of endorphins,
surge of my being bursting forth,
the relief from sleepy nights smothering soot at home top
and the fear of trespassing terraces leaves with creaking bicycles
round the corner.
Times of phoenixes that die, die and die...
Soar, awake, again in haste and for hearts brimming to lay bare a
saga of the newly old before life fits in binaries, again.

Pulses and Impulses

Shadows knock on the door even when you fold the
hinge and close the blinds.
Strobing before being invaded by lights at dawn,
gurgling like the stream that keeps away foam but not quite.
Brimming over and into exhausted syllables of disease.
Here, over and into are indeed two sides of the
same rowing process.
You try to peep into reflections that break iron
gates without poise.
Who can blame impulses at the altar of no-constancy?
The philosophy of history is one beyond guns and laurels but still
one none the same where cowards canter away without noise.
Past was never for the weak.
Revisiting isn't just some truth-tryst with memories nor
remembrance bitter pulses that untimely soar and peak.

The floodgates try closing each time and fail with your resolve to
volunteer inundation. The singularity of trials gouges out your eyes.
And you, re-utter love is light when it's grave right at its core,
fertile and replete with texts that you half parrot to wipe away
meaning. "Every careless word makes you love a little less", says a
poetess

who didn't know that carelessness is sort of spontaneity with
denial or some suppose that proximity is a mess.
That words, though careless, cares about its owner.
The terrible agony of the horns flutters away rides after they had
sped past through blind alleys.
Past the drowsy and pathetic loner.

So, shadows knock on floodgates when they falter.
Don't blame the latches or the anger of the waves.
They are just fine at impulses rave.
Pulses often purge in spaces that die or cave.

Hour of the Deaf

This breeze at sunrise is chilly in its remembrances of dirt on sickly collars.
Like stars that hide their shine within a few hours of unease.
There's more life in circuits of the mechanical head than in trains and rails.
Scraping through meanings in cubist frames of thought after a hard day's labour and running over pages of non-sense lyrics.
The politics of it is in lighting up a volcano and trying to wrestle with it to its death with daybreak.
In yet another re-vision of where desires should end
And you cull out mistakes in keeping time and killing it long after still the hour of the deaf.

A Winter Passes By

Till the mellow flowers wilt in tonight,
and the rude stomps try crushing dew-daubed pebbles
Keep burning the bell-jar as it melts without breaking.
There's so little to stories that transpire in secrecy and die
unburied deaths.
Through weeks and months there's one time contesting against
itself
Peeping to look in between your urge and habit and at
where it slips;
keeping no tale before you know of an art where all must fall.
Words too must die secret deaths before they fade into the
horizon of token speech and embryonic calls. But believe there
will be time, not Eliotian.
There will be time for more sleep and little adieu, for summer to
come and for blooms anew.

Habit

Nerves aren't really a bundle, they come each raw
each with their throbs. Blotting out consciousness from time.
Edging out reality is no child's play. But hold the shingles dry in your palms
till they stone you in turn. And the sea-salted air of intimacy
steams into half dreamt starry nights.
It becomes a habit sometimes to steal before it strikes the clock.
It becomes a habit too to talk under the hollow lights.
A habit to respond and love when you are invited to mossy quarters before your initiation
Till you let the tune take you out of your sight.
Till verses are conversations are routines are where you oblige.
So, your nerves relax, relax and contract or keep changing the rhyme and missing the flight.
Don't let them search for the workings between impulses and meaning
Lest the rawness finds none of it at all to court words from indexes while they struggle and fight.
The clock will strike the beat and with time hear it chime.
While you give yourself to the habits of others, habit your habit to look within and thaw.

25 Times

Always an easy task to breathe but not to 'be',
Nor to 'be' in a way where you try to really breathe.
Look at simpler tangents out of your curtains and teach life from life, or talk to yourself all the time till you know what you need.
You will not know always what you need. So don't try counting every seed
that you sowed by your hand.
But look at the trout swimming uphill, no trailblazer though it knows how to curve its way through currents it doesn't understand.
And that hummingbird building its nest, close to the bough on which it thought it could but not land.
No, forests aren't really that dark at night, but it feels abysmal for ages till you pass it on to your hindsight.
And views from peaks are often lonely but those below stifling.
So, chart out your course away from the league if you might.

Love till its love, blind yourself forward when it's not and question questions even if they questioned once what ought to be fought.
For you will not miss people or places alone, apart from themselves, individually, onto their own stations.
But what you and I will run after, always, are situations.

Unintention

So, if you believe it all starts with words
let them coil up and cut through the pieces of haste,
and tremble on a winter night like this. Alone but secure.
They are not ready to be baked beside ashes
that you willingly choose for your every night's sleep.
Light the fire again. Let the trembling melt along dissonances
within yourself and beyond.
So, what if it ripples through the statis of near luxury? These are
times you don't want rhyme to forge a pattern onto the senses of
the page. So, there's the play ill-chalked out.
The play is fast but the effects slow
as it slowly seeps into the bones of time and rises to infirmity.
This infirmity is precious and potent. Infirmity right at the face
of eternity and its woes.
To hold back words that they never know how to run. How to
live, plead or bow.

Winter Tale

This withering of time and the descent of night
Life moves in circles.
And exhaustion is no exhausted lie.
To begin a winter tale is counter-intuitive.
Close your mind and live before you bury what would die.

UnMind

So sometimes when in love
Believe in no death or respite
where the souls aren't easily begotten
there are more phantoms to what you perceive in your robe
Lest you give a ride to your mind forgotten
that reining in is an act of the brave and so fight
where your mind fails you without the shove.

Philosopher

To mornings that don't meet your eye
But poise in eternal recurrence.
Forget Nietzsche for a moment.
And see where lies the lie.
Value creation is not a myth though sometimes it doesn't make sense.

Another Year

The boxes and the brains
Hoppers before sunrise and between little few lines of use.
Love comes in many forms in a year accursed.
Marking steps while you toast on days that take away less than what you would give.
Recount losses as you sleep off before the dead
Or look behind a year's ruse.

Fascists and Fascists.

We, the people, not so collective
Calibrating democracy, year after year
speaking truth to power,
talking about the 'post-truth' and the 'hyper-real'
thinking and re-thinking what shouldn't bind us to cells
that do not allow circles of light-drops.
Rushing through diction, fiction and idioms.
Swimming onto the traces of the political'.

The political states that we are not a collective
and *I* need *You* different to breathe and *You* need *Me* hostile.
And *I* will search for many 'I's while *you* search for your '*You*'s
and let us collide.
Till your '*You*'s vaporize into my '*I*'s. But I need it before my
eyes, all before my eyes till *I* know we are enough to
now
find newer '*You*'s within *Us*.

We pledge to hear *Us*, *you and me*,
finding politics
in life.
And in finding it we are a collective

On roads and rails.
Some days, *I* invite *Us* into my room where *I* preserve my difference and leave space for *You* to be *You.*
We will celebrate it in art and discourse
through our words and smiles till *we* turn back and thunder in closed hands of how that *You* in *you* is disturbing.
That the grudges of the 'enlightenment' and the 'revolutionary' spared *you* both ways
and for *You* my pity churns till it makes me true democratic.

Each *You* and *I* pen the same thing down every night before we glow through the discourses of life and art.
Clapping each *I* to silence.
We talk of difference next day and cut out the fuss
There lies a fascist in each one of *Us*.

Vision

The glare of those neons.
shimmering attire, living, loving, laughing. The bustle of the street, the
thoroughfares of festivity, the salty smell of *pakoras* and your eyes spare a
second round the corner.
You realise that the dish in your hand wasn't as vapid anymore.
The salt in the air has found its way to morph its state. In rivulets
they trickle down some old, forgotten ways.
But a few still await release.
What still confounds them in those potholes of arid wilderness?
No hope but immunity, may be a flickering whim of chances.
The dusty curs howl all the same; silence smears the other nook.
People live, laugh. Ignorance grasps love.

Sea-Side

When each foot measures a distant toil,
numerous whispers muffle aloud heartbreaks,
the nights descend to comfort and foil,
human ambitions that leave by but streaks...
streaks of glitter and gold
days of impatience scuffing their ways…
ways that are drudged but bold
with divisive musings surfacing to the fore, you glance at them
you keep on dreaming
They ruffle and roar.

Rhythm

A stack of papers
a sigh or breath
a voyage through time, sprawling darkness
Fading smiles, lost moments,
simple regrets, weakening failures, withering ties, hopeless secrets.
And still,
Familiar faces, implied language... scattered pieces, languid sketches ...an hour of montage.
"But what is this? It is not what I was looking for."
"It is that you have been, the unborn."

Mirror Stage

Every time you attempt to pull it back
In a rage will it emerge
Every trick you do with it, pushing it to the cliff's verge
Will meet a tempestuous entity
That had never known to break or bow
With every paralytic function that you fetter the wings with, be sure, there shall be an upward surge.
Learn to bear with it, my friend.
It's not my time neither yours, but it'll make all your horizons blend with mine soon, all your qualms with my conviction shall shortly merge.

Pisces

Words multiply, writhe and cry
revelations upon revelations; "think! think!", thus says the 'sage'
Revelations are done, loud disasters with great re-'vision'
"Look, look!" says his slanted sight, the other half dreams of
dreaming, dreams to break and mock yours and mine
I don't laugh or despise when he 'educates' masses in each season
just wink an eye through his guise and fly
Or sing when he rises in rage.

Dead Connect

Between those invisible moments of silence,
You gratefully urge for conference that blows in my uncollected guilt.
Our words resort to the violence of metaphors that mean not what we think but I try catching the openness of analogies. Off within known pulses and intensities.
You wrap your senses with the phantom of my indifference while I harbour muted thoughts and exhaust them with poor, cold, tawny experiences.
Deadness is a rare function, livid and beautiful.
I urge you this time, like every day.
To stay more with this dreaded deferral, what if our voices disperse and defect.
I still spare my life beyond; I try to live through this dead connect.

Year End

Here, again I try counting (on)
Minutes minutely, years apart, every-year, every-man.
With moist fingertips, the broken rod of balance is elusive to feel.
Adapting hasn't been its screw.
Failed numerals and irrationality are somewhat parallel within maths and philosophy.
I feel it. I haven't learnt it though. The year had been one of suppositions.
So (suppose) you can only float indefinitely in your niche.
Suppose elasticity, always, has some broken base underneath. It does not assess definite collages every year.
So, my 'spine' is more elastic than you think from your overcharged territories. I think I can't have it broken through an excessive sway each time nor freeze it erect, senseless.
I will let it move.
I will love from afar the girl I don't admit caring for. No, not your hopeless romantic. I will keep that elastic too. Both full and draughty at times. Adapting is a virtue like no other but it engulfs elasticity.
So, I silently let it drop in between the setbacks and celebrations of each revision.

Of every encounter, (suppose), I have looked for expansion in all its extending and contracting moments.

Say between al frenzy and feelings of loss.

Between al equity and duplicity, I shall (suppose) locate the median within acts.

Still Love

There lacks continuity, no grit in me but say,
the day you looked at me looking away before a winter sun;
the only decadence lay in the dwindling twilight.
Mist and leafless trees an expiring flame and a companion,
a fit too dear for a broken heart., a clock too tired to test its
might against numerous alarms put to snooze. You are really
strange, earthly as the moss suffusing the area of the clay,
adamant to annex the sod yet greeting with denials to pay the
price of a pervading root.
The words could never flow nor shoot its aim. Yours has been a
strange game, a game neither of gambles nor of cards. but one
that chars the theories of probability,
that alone sets contrition loose.
The verses could never flow, your failing dam was the nail I gave
up on before hooking the frame. So, try me another time dear
love, for I won't stay here long.
But the affection that imperils you to frailty is a blame that
mustn't be my song.
Your being chill is no comfortable dry day, but dodging
commitment was never my way to mar your hours of belonging,
a touch never made or say a wish evaded on purpose to keep
whims at bay. For days will morph into speeding months, but let
me seek respite, once if I may.

Awake

Numbness in your senses, your inability to confide;
they say it's illusion, an angst beneath the tide
And drilling into it you suppose, "the epistemic violence will cease"
But surely no hope into that, no comfort, no ease.
And treading round the clock, you know not how to run
Let the mirage burn you then, for 'truth' remains more impure, monstrous not to shun.

Trial

I had tried to fit in.
The meshes of your dualities
To choose weeds and ferns or chase the hilly terrain.
I have come to know weeds grow in slopes too.
That all blinks are not points of dices.
That your dulcet tune is often absorbing but centrifuge has always been my pipe.
I won't be your moon or the sun, they come by turns.
I am in love with those clouds. That though intercepts, seeks to bother none

No Closure

Without a few letters stand demanding erasure,
thoughts in drops may, now, bleed
Here the tussle dives far beyond the comical
to a point of stuttering rhythmic violence
Before you try reaching the thresholds of 'choice' or 'dissidence'
Nothing looks sober or base in the extra-canonical reading of self
or its need
Or where a cubist miniature of images debates some kind of
closure.

Before Daybreak

But language has often been terrible in its unmaking
Of once-written dirges and symphonies against re-visiting talks
And I have lived nights (like this) conveying silence.
Doubting inability at my manhood, stroking off figures with white;
Those that have refused to bear traces within a word, solemn, or may be made in jest;
Awaiting resolution like my fingers till daybreak.

One Un-Poetry

It's a farce to know not where poetry begins
At the loss of language or
with the language of loss,
Having crept through every familiar thought
and pinning darts at the dead cross.
Or stuffing what you sneer at as the only embryonic truth.
Words have given the lie to theory, today, up on foot.
You ask me what made me take oaths that I could never bear?
Of muting silence through careless words.
Cascading and rippling through everything that was not meant to be fear.
At times even
Blind by eyes I have lived wrong.
Saved judgment too late
And still judged wrong.
And yet...
I long for all those I hated and dreamt to escape from.
These are phases that you detest when you revise with your boiling pulse.
Look, I have cried through scores of un-starry nights.
Don't fall for me then.
There is no language weaved within me. I pen un-poetry.
I ain't your stereotypical man.